CANADA

Ginger McDonnell

Table of Contents

Welcome to Canada!   3

Plants   10

Animals   12

Sports   14

More About Canada   18

Glossary   20

Welcome to Canada!

Welcome to Canada, the North American country nearest the North Pole!

Today Canada is its own country. Long ago, it belonged to England. Before that it belonged to France.

The 5 Biggest Countries in the World

1. Russia
2. Canada
3. China
4. United States
5. Brazil

Canada is the second biggest country in the world by size. It covers most of the top of North America.

Native Americans were the first people living in Canada. Canada's name comes from a Native American word for "village."

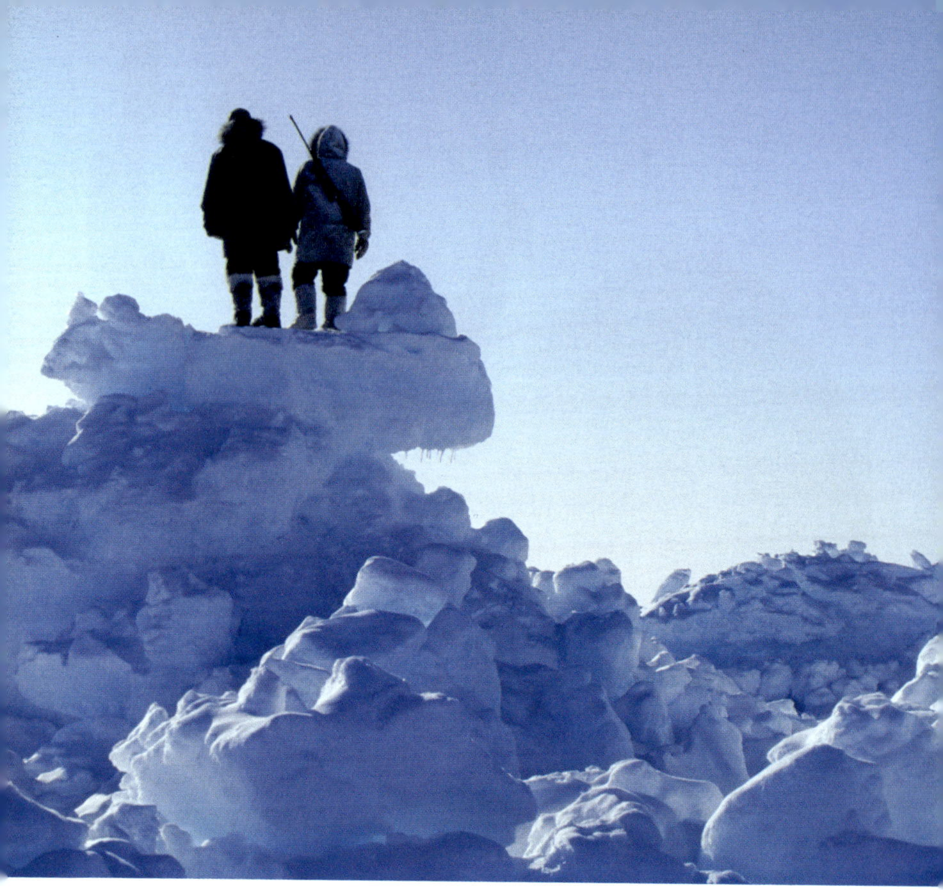

Some of the world's prettiest land is in Canada.

The north of Canada is very cold. It is often covered with snow and ice. Few people live there.

Canada has deep, green forests. It also has tall, rocky mountains. Mount Logan is the tallest mountain of all.

There are many islands in Canada. Sandy shores, green meadows, and colorful wildflowers can be found there.

Farms stretch under big,
blue skies across Canada's wide
plains.

Plants

The plains have few trees but a lot of tall prairie grass. There are almost no plants in the north.

10

In the west, thick forests are filled with evergreens like pine, spruce, and fir.

Have you ever smelled an evergreen forest? It has a rich, spicy smell.

Animals

Different animals live in each kind of land. In the forests you will find wolves, rabbits, and beavers. Deer, foxes, and bears live there, too.

Furry polar bears and caribou love the chilly north. Narwhals like the cold ocean there.

Sports

Canada is well known for winter sports. Hockey is a favorite sport there. Canada has some of the best hockey teams in the world.

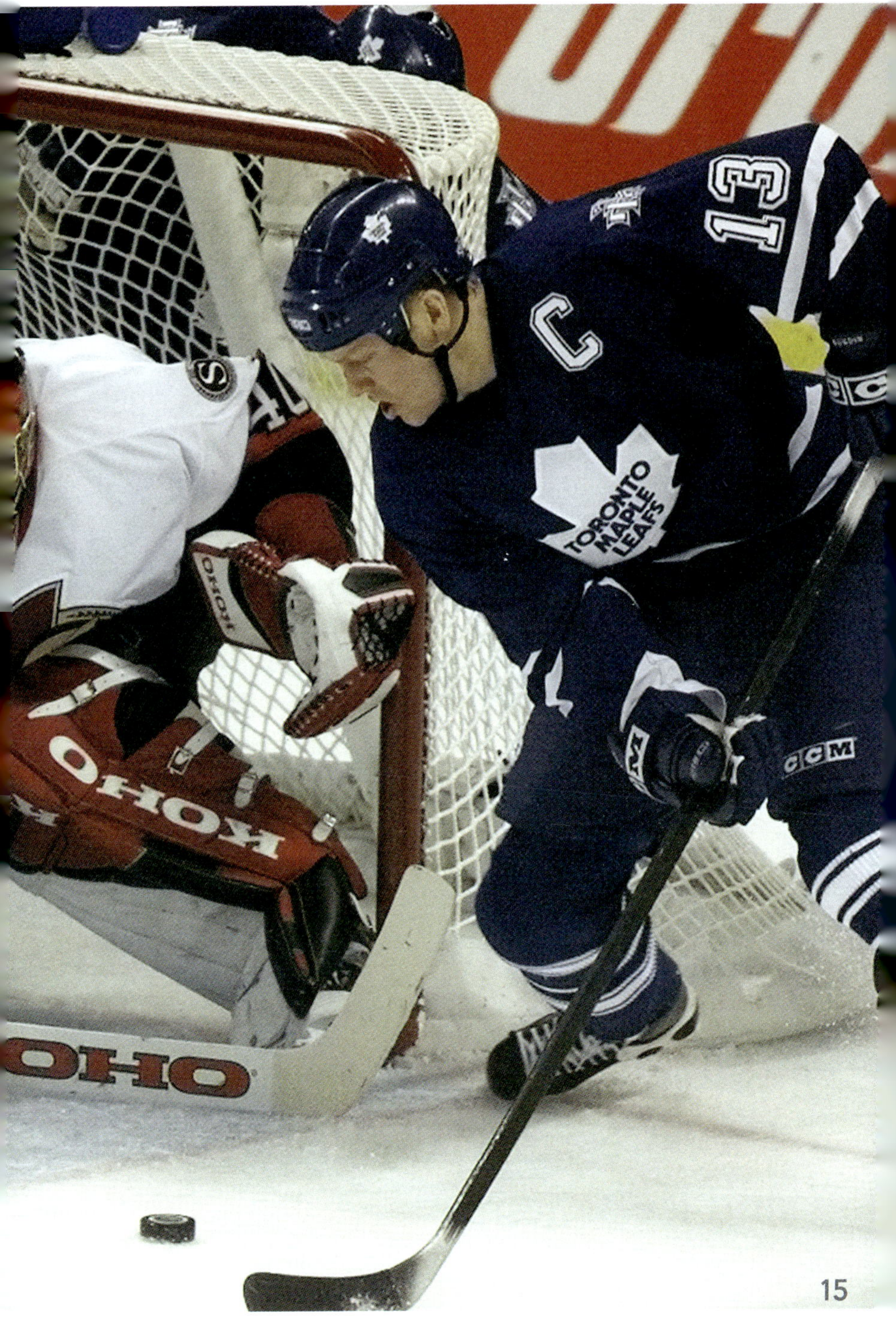
13
TORONTO
MAPLE
LEAFS
CCM

Canadian athletes often do well in the Winter Olympics. They are especially good skiers and ice skaters.

16

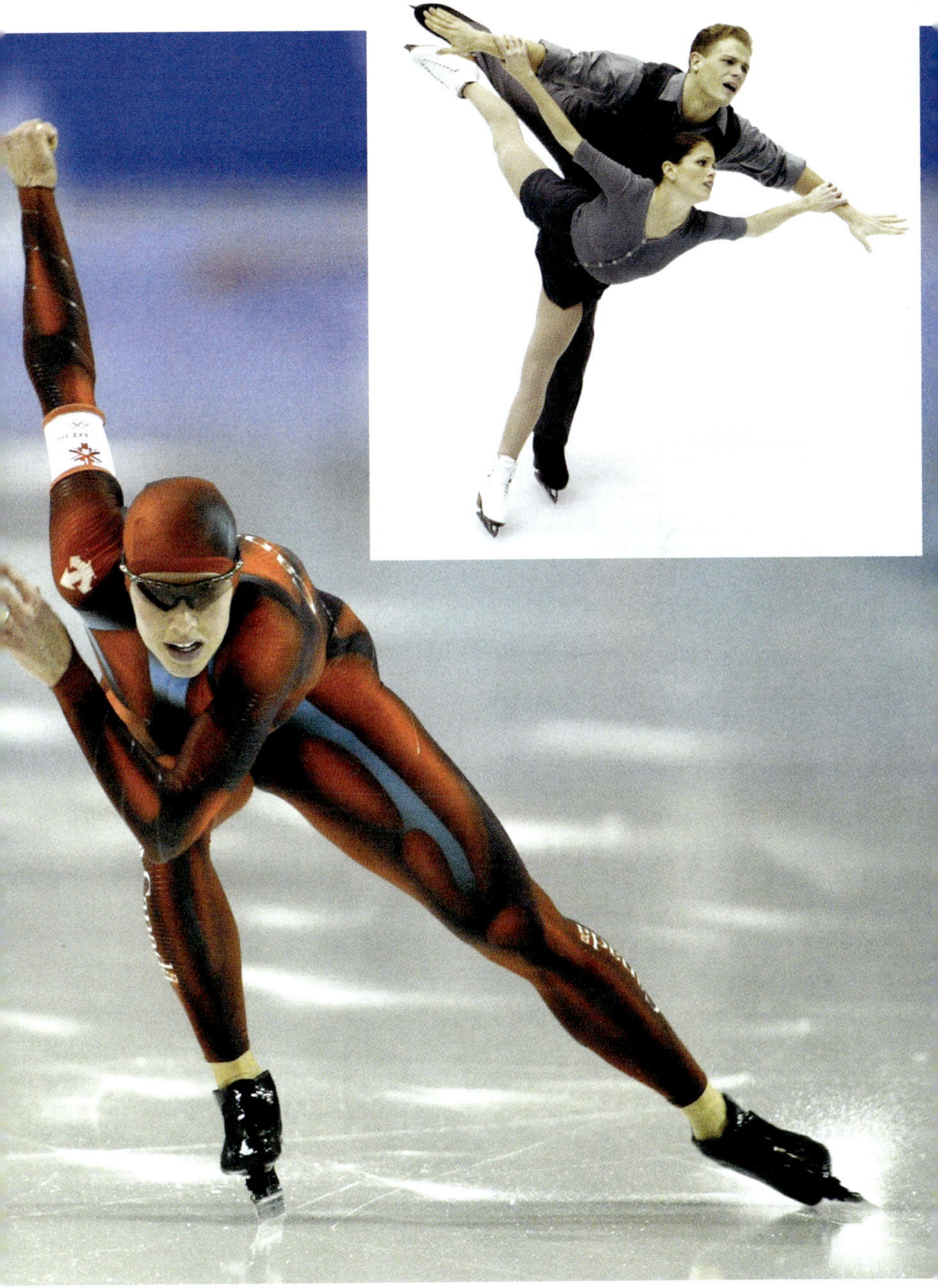

More About Canada

There are many big cities in Canada. Toronto is the biggest city. Ottawa is Canada's capital.

Montréal is an old city. Most people there speak French, just like the people who settled there long ago.

What else would you like to know about Canada? This chart will tell you more important facts.

Canadian Facts

Official Languages:	English and French
Leader:	Prime Minister
Year of Independence:	1931
Number of Provinces:	10
Number of Territories:	3
Flag:	3 stripes (red, white, red); red maple leaf in the center
Symbol:	maple leaf
Anthem:	"O, Canada"
Major Crops:	wheat, barley, potatoes, corn, soybeans
Money:	Canadian dollar

19

Glossary

Canada a large country in North America

caribou a type of deer that lives in the arctic

evergreen a kind of plant that is green all year round

forests areas of land with large, thick growths of trees

hockey a sport played on ice with sticks and a puck

meadows areas of land covered with grass

narwhals a type of whale that lives in arctic oceans

Native American people whose ancestors were the first to live in the Americas

North America one of the seven continents of the world

plains treeless open areas of land

prairie a wide area of rolling grassland

shores land along the edges of bodies of water

Winter Olympics sport competitions played every four years by athletes from around the world